MW00881340

Internet address
&
Password logbook

Network Setup

Home network settings

Broadband modem

Model:

Serial number:

MAC address:

Administration URL/IP address:

WAN IP address:

Username:

Password:

Router/Wireless access point

Model:

Serial number:

Default IP Address:

Default username:

Default password:

User defined IP address:

User defined username:

User defined password:

WAN settings

MAC address:

IP address: _____

Host name: _____

Domain name: _____

Subnet mask: _____

Default gateway: _____

DNS -- primary: _____

DNS -- secondary: _____

LAN settings _____

IP address: _____

Subnet mask: _____

DHCP range: _____

Wireless settings _____

SSID (Network name): _____

Channel: _____

Security mode: _____

Shared key (WPA): _____

Passphrase (WEP): _____

Internet & Computer Information

ISP name:

Account number:

Tech support:

Customer service:

Email (personal):

Mail server type:

Incoming server:

Outgoing server:

Username:

Password:

Email (work):

Mail server type:

Incoming server:

Outgoing server:

Username:

Password:

Domain:

Passwords

A

Name:

Site address:

Login/username:

Password:

Notes:

Name:

Site address:

Login/username:

Password:

Notes:

Name:

Site address:

Login/username:

Password:

Notes:

Name:

Site address:

Login/username:

Password:

Notes:

Name:

Site address:

Login/username:

Password:

Notes:

Name:

Site address:

Login/username:

Password:

Notes:

Name:

Site address:

Login/username:

Password:

Notes:

Name:

Site address:

Login/username:

Password:

Notes:

Name:

Site address:

Login/username:

Password:

Notes:

Name:

Site address:

Login/username:

Password:

Notes:

Name:

Site address:

Login/username:

Password:

Notes:

Name:

Site address:

Login/username:

Password:

Notes:

Name:

Site address:

Login/username:

Password:

Notes:

Name:

Site address:

Login/username:

Password:

Notes:

Name:

Site address:

Login/username:

Password:

Notes:

Name:

Site address:

Login/username:

Password:

Notes:

Name:

Site address:

Login/username:

Password:

Notes:

Name:

Site address:

Login/username:

Password:

Notes:

Name:

Site address:

Login/username:

Password:

Notes:

Name:

Site address:

Login/username:

Password:

Notes:

Name:

Site address:

Login/username:

Password:

Notes:

Name:

Site address:

Login/username:

Password:

Notes:

Name:

Site address:

Login/username:

Password:

Notes:

Name:

Site address:

Login/username:

Password:

Notes:

Name:

Site address:

Login/username:

Password:

Notes:

Name:

Site address:

Login/username:

Password:

Notes:

Name:

Site address:

Login/username:

Password:

Notes:

Name:

Site address:

Login/username:

Password:

Notes:

Name:

Site address:

Login/username:

Password:

Notes:

Name:

Site address:

Login/username:

Password:

Notes:

Name:

Site address:

Login/username:

Password:

Notes:

Name:

Site address:

Login/username:

Password:

Notes:

Name:

Site address:

Login/username:

Password:

Notes:

Name:

Site address:

Login/username:

Password:

Notes:

Name:

Site address:

Login/username:

Password:

Notes:

Name:

Site address:

Login/username:

Password:

Notes:

Name:

Site address:

Login/username:

Password:

Notes:

Name:

Site address:

Login/username:

Password:

Notes:

Name:

Site address:

Login/username:

Password:

Notes:

Name:

Site address:

Login/username:

Password:

Notes:

Name:

Site address:

Login/username:

Password:

Notes:

Name:

Site address:

Login/username:

Password:

Notes:

Name:

Site address:

Login/username:

Password:

Notes:

Name:

Site address:

Login/username:

Password:

Notes:

Name:

Site address:

Login/username:

Password:

Notes:

Name:

Site address:

Login/username:

Password:

Notes:

Name:

Site address:

Login/username:

Password:

Notes:

Name:

Site address:

Login/username:

Password:

Notes:

Name:

Site address:

Login/username:

Password:

Notes:

Name:

Site address:

Login/username:

Password:

Notes:

Name:

Site address:

Login/username:

Password:

Notes:

Name:

Site address:

Login/username:

Password:

Notes:

Name:

Site address:

Login/username:

Password:

Notes:

Name:

Site address:

Login/username:

Password:

Notes:

Name:

Site address:

Login/username:

Password:

Notes:

Name:

Site address:

Login/username:

Password:

Notes:

Name:

Site address:

Login/username:

Password:

Notes:

E

Name:

Site address:

Login/username:

Password:

Notes:

Name:

Site address:

Login/username:

Password:

Notes:

Name:

Site address:

Login/username:

Password:

Notes:

Name:

Site address:

Login/username:

Password:

Notes:

Name:

Site address:

Login/username:

Password:

Notes:

Name:

Site address:

Login/username:

Password:

Notes:

Name:

Site address:

Login/username:

Password:

Notes:

Name:

Site address:

Login/username:

Password:

Notes:

Name:

Site address:

Login/username:

Password:

Notes:

Name:

Site address:

Login/username:

Password:

Notes:

Name:

Site address:

Login/username:

Password:

Notes:

Name:

Site address:

Login/username:

Password:

Notes:

Name:

Site address:

Login/username:

Password:

Notes:

Name:

Site address:

Login/username:

Password:

Notes:

Name:

Site address:

Login/username:

Password:

Notes:

Name:

Site address:

Login/username:

Password:

Notes:

Name:

Site address:

Login/username:

Password:

Notes:

Name:

Site address:

Login/username:

Password:

Notes:

Name:

Site address:

Login/username:

Password:

Notes:

Name:

Site address:

Login/username:

Password:

Notes:

Name:

Site address:

Login/username:

Password:

Notes:

Name:

Site address:

Login/username:

Password:

Notes:

Name:

Site address:

Login/username:

Password:

Notes:

Name:

Site address:

Login/username:

Password:

Notes:

Name:

Site address:

Login/username:

Password:

Notes:

Name:

Site address:

Login/username:

Password:

Notes:

Name:

Site address:

Login/username:

Password:

Notes:

H

Name:

Site address:

Login/username:

Password:

Notes:

Name:

Site address:

Login/username:

Password:

Notes:

Name:

Site address:

Login/username:

Password:

Notes:

Name:

Site address:

Login/username:

Password:

Notes:

Name:

Site address:

Login/username:

Password:

Notes:

Name:

Site address:

Login/username:

Password:

Notes:

Name:

Site address:

Login/username:

Password:

Notes:

Name:

Site address:

Login/username:

Password:

Notes:

Name:

Site address:

Login/username:

Password:

Notes:

Name: _____

Site address: _____

Login/username: _____

Password: _____

Notes: _____

_____

_____

Name: _____

Site address: _____

Login/username: _____

Password: _____

Notes: _____

_____

_____

Name: _____

Site address: _____

Login/username: _____

Password: _____

Notes: _____

_____

_____

Name:

Site address:

Login/username:

Password:

Notes:

Name:

Site address:

Login/username:

Password:

Notes:

Name:

Site address:

Login/username:

Password:

Notes:

Name:

Site address:

Login/username:

Password:

Notes:

Name:

Site address:

Login/username:

Password:

Notes:

Name:

Site address:

Login/username:

Password:

Notes:

Name:

Site address:

Login/username:

Password:

Notes:

Name:

Site address:

Login/username:

Password:

Notes:

Name:

Site address:

Login/username:

Password:

Notes:

Name:

Site address:

Login/username:

Password:

Notes:

Name:

Site address:

Login/username:

Password:

Notes:

Name:

Site address:

Login/username:

Password:

Notes:

Name:

Site address:

Login/username:

Password:

Notes:

Name:

Site address:

Login/username:

Password:

Notes:

Name:

Site address:

Login/username:

Password:

Notes:

Name:

Site address:

Login/username:

Password:

Notes:

Name:

Site address:

Login/username:

Password:

Notes:

Name:

Site address:

Login/username:

Password:

Notes:

Name:

Site address:

Login/username:

Password:

Notes:

Name:

Site address:

Login/username:

Password:

Notes:

Name:

Site address:

Login/username:

Password:

Notes:

Name:

Site address:

Login/username:

Password:

Notes:

Name:

Site address:

Login/username:

Password:

Notes:

Name:

Site address:

Login/username:

Password:

Notes:

L

Name:

Site address:

Login/username:

Password:

Notes:

Name:

Site address:

Login/username:

Password:

Notes:

Name:

Site address:

Login/username:

Password:

Notes:

Name:

Site address:

Login/username:

Password:

Notes:

Name:

Site address:

Login/username:

Password:

Notes:

Name:

Site address:

Login/username:

Password:

Notes:

Name:

Site address:

Login/username:

Password:

Notes:

Name:

Site address:

Login/username:

Password:

Notes:

Name:

Site address:

Login/username:

Password:

Notes:

Name:

Site address:

Login/username:

Password:

Notes:

Name:

Site address:

Login/username:

Password:

Notes:

Name:

Site address:

Login/username:

Password:

Notes:

Name:

Site address:

Login/username:

Password:

Notes:

Name:

Site address:

Login/username:

Password:

Notes:

Name:

Site address:

Login/username:

Password:

Notes:

Name:

Site address:

Login/username:

Password:

Notes:

Name:

Site address:

Login/username:

Password:

Notes:

Name:

Site address:

Login/username:

Password:

Notes:

Name:

Site address:

Login/username:

Password:

Notes:

Name:

Site address:

Login/username:

Password:

Notes:

Name:

Site address:

Login/username:

Password:

Notes:

Name:

Site address:

Login/username:

Password:

Notes:

Name:

Site address:

Login/username:

Password:

Notes:

Name:

Site address:

Login/username:

Password:

Notes:

Name:

Site address:

Login/username:

Password:

Notes:

Name:

Site address:

Login/username:

Password:

Notes:

Name:

Site address:

Login/username:

Password:

Notes:

Name:

Site address:

Login/username:

Password:

Notes:

Name:

Site address:

Login/username:

Password:

Notes:

Name:

Site address:

Login/username:

Password:

Notes:

Name:

Site address:

Login/username:

Password:

Notes:

Name:

Site address:

Login/username:

Password:

Notes:

Name:

Site address:

Login/username:

Password:

Notes:

N

Name:

Site address:

Login/username:

Password:

Notes:

Name:

Site address:

Login/username:

Password:

Notes:

Name:

Site address:

Login/username:

Password:

Notes:

Name:

Site address:

Login/username:

Password:

Notes:

Name:

Site address:

Login/username:

Password:

Notes:

Name:

Site address:

Login/username:

Password:

Notes:

Name:

Site address:

Login/username:

Password:

Notes:

Name:

Site address:

Login/username:

Password:

Notes:

Name:

Site address:

Login/username:

Password:

Notes:

Name:

Site address:

Login/username:

Password:

Notes:

Name:

Site address:

Login/username:

Password:

Notes:

Name:

Site address:

Login/username:

Password:

Notes:

Name:

Site address:

Login/username:

Password:

Notes:

Name:

Site address:

Login/username:

Password:

Notes:

Name:

Site address:

Login/username:

Password:

Notes:

P

Name:

Site address:

Login/username:

Password:

Notes:

Name:

Site address:

Login/username:

Password:

Notes:

Name:

Site address:

Login/username:

Password:

Notes:

P

Name:

Site address:

Login/username:

Password:

Notes:

Name:

Site address:

Login/username:

Password:

Notes:

Name:

Site address:

Login/username:

Password:

Notes:

Name:

Site address:

Login/username:

Password:

Notes:

Name:

Site address:

Login/username:

Password:

Notes:

Name:

Site address:

Login/username:

Password:

Notes:

Name:

Site address:

Login/username:

Password:

Notes:

Name:

Site address:

Login/username:

Password:

Notes:

Name:

Site address:

Login/username:

Password:

Notes:

Name:

Site address:

Login/username:

Password:

Notes:

Name:

Site address:

Login/username:

Password:

Notes:

Name:

Site address:

Login/username:

Password:

Notes:

Name:

Site address:

Login/username:

Password:

Notes:

Name:

Site address:

Login/username:

Password:

Notes:

Name:

Site address:

Login/username:

Password:

Notes:

Name:

Site address:

Login/username:

Password:

Notes:

Name:

Site address:

Login/username:

Password:

Notes:

Name:

Site address:

Login/username:

Password:

Notes:

Name:

Site address:

Login/username:

Password:

Notes:

Name:

Site address:

Login/username:

Password:

Notes:

Name:

Site address:

Login/username:

Password:

Notes:

Name:

Site address:

Login/username:

Password:

Notes:

Name:

Site address:

Login/username:

Password:

Notes:

Name:

Site address:

Login/username:

Password:

Notes:

Name:

Site address:

Login/username:

Password:

Notes:

Name:

Site address:

Login/username:

Password:

Notes:

Name:

Site address:

Login/username:

Password:

Notes:

Name:

Site address:

Login/username:

Password:

Notes:

Name:

Site address:

Login/username:

Password:

Notes:

Name:

Site address:

Login/username:

Password:

Notes:

S

Name:

Site address:

Login/username:

Password:

Notes:

Name:

Site address:

Login/username:

Password:

Notes:

Name:

Site address:

Login/username:

Password:

Notes:

Name:

Site address:

Login/username:

Password:

Notes:

Name:

Site address:

Login/username:

Password:

Notes:

Name:

Site address:

Login/username:

Password:

Notes:

Name:

Site address:

Login/username:

Password:

Notes:

Name:

Site address:

Login/username:

Password:

Notes:

Name:

Site address:

Login/username:

Password:

Notes:

Name:

Site address:

Login/username:

Password:

Notes:

Name:

Site address:

Login/username:

Password:

Notes:

Name:

Site address:

Login/username:

Password:

Notes:

Name:

Site address:

Login/username:

Password:

Notes:

Name:

Site address:

Login/username:

Password:

Notes:

Name:

Site address:

Login/username:

Password:

Notes:

Name:

Site address:

Login/username:

Password:

Notes:

Name:

Site address:

Login/username:

Password:

Notes:

Name:

Site address:

Login/username:

Password:

Notes:

Name:

Site address:

Login/username:

Password:

Notes:

Name:

Site address:

Login/username:

Password:

Notes:

Name:

Site address:

Login/username:

Password:

Notes:

Name:

Site address:

Login/username:

Password:

Notes:

Name:

Site address:

Login/username:

Password:

Notes:

Name:

Site address:

Login/username:

Password:

Notes:

Name:

Site address:

Login/username:

Password:

Notes:

Name:

Site address:

Login/username:

Password:

Notes:

Name:

Site address:

Login/username:

Password:

Notes:

Name:

Site address:

Login/username:

Password:

Notes:

Name:

Site address:

Login/username:

Password:

Notes:

Name:

Site address:

Login/username:

Password:

Notes:

Name:

Site address:

Login/username:

Password:

Notes:

Name:

Site address:

Login/username:

Password:

Notes:

Name:

Site address:

Login/username:

Password:

Notes:

W

Name:

Site address:

Login/username:

Password:

Notes:

Name:

Site address:

Login/username:

Password:

Notes:

Name:

Site address:

Login/username:

Password:

Notes:

W

Name:

Site address:

Login/username:

Password:

Notes:

Name:

Site address:

Login/username:

Password:

Notes:

Name:

Site address:

Login/username:

Password:

Notes:

Name:

Site address:

Login/username:

Password:

Notes:

Name:

Site address:

Login/username:

Password:

Notes:

Name:

Site address:

Login/username:

Password:

Notes:

Name:

Site address:

Login/username:

Password:

Notes:

Name:

Site address:

Login/username:

Password:

Notes:

Name:

Site address:

Login/username:

Password:

Notes:

Name:

Site address:

Login/username:

Password:

Notes:

Name:

Site address:

Login/username:

Password:

Notes:

Name:

Site address:

Login/username:

Password:

Notes:

Name:

Site address:

Login/username:

Password:

Notes:

Name:

Site address:

Login/username:

Password:

Notes:

Name:

Site address:

Login/username:

Password:

Notes:

Name:

Site address:

Login/username:

Password:

Notes:

Name:

Site address:

Login/username:

Password:

Notes:

Name:

Site address:

Login/username:

Password:

Notes:

Name:

Site address:

Login/username:

Password:

Notes:

Name:

Site address:

Login/username:

Password:

Notes:

Name:

Site address:

Login/username:

Password:

Notes:

Name:

Site address:

Login/username:

Password:

Notes:

Name:

Site address:

Login/username:

Password:

Notes:

Name:

Site address:

Login/username:

Password:

Notes:

Name:

Site address:

Login/username:

Password:

Notes:

Name:

Site address:

Login/username:

Password:

Notes:

Name:

Site address:

Login/username:

Password:

Notes:

Name:

Site address:

Login/username:

Password:

Notes:

Name:

Site address:

Login/username:

Password:

Notes:

Name:

Site address:

Login/username:

Password:

Notes:

Z

Name:

Site address:

Login/username:

Password:

Notes:

Name:

Site address:

Login/username:

Password:

Notes:

Name:

Site address:

Login/username:

Password:

Notes:

Z

Name:

Site address:

Login/username:

Password:

Notes:

Name:

Site address:

Login/username:

Password:

Notes:

Name:

Site address:

Login/username:

Password:

Notes:

Z

Name:

Site address:

Login/username:

Password:

Notes:

Name:

Site address:

Login/username:

Password:

Notes:

Name:

Site address:

Login/username:

Password:

Notes:

Name:

Site address:

Login/username:

Password:

Notes:

Name:

Site address:

Login/username:

Password:

Notes:

Name:

Site address:

Login/username:

Password:

Notes:

Name:

Site address:

Login/username:

Password:

Notes:

Name:

Site address:

Login/username:

Password:

Notes:

Name:

Site address:

Login/username:

Password:

Notes:

Name:

Site address:

Login/username:

Password:

Notes:

Name:

Site address:

Login/username:

Password:

Notes:

Name:

Site address:

Login/username:

Password:

Notes:

Z

Name:

Site address:

Login/username:

Password:

Notes:

Name:

Site address:

Login/username:

Password:

Notes:

Name:

Site address:

Login/username:

Password:

Notes:

Name:

Site address:

Login/username:

Password:

Notes:

Name:

Site address:

Login/username:

Password:

Notes:

Name:

Site address:

Login/username:

Password:

Notes:

Name:

Site address:

Login/username:

Password:

Notes:

Name:

Site address:

Login/username:

Password:

Notes:

Name:

Site address:

Login/username:

Password:

Notes:

Name:

Site address:

Login/username:

Password:

Notes:

Name:

Site address:

Login/username:

Password:

Notes:

Name:

Site address:

Login/username:

Password:

Notes:

Made in United States
Orlando, FL
28 April 2024

46242656R00064